Heinrich Karl Brugsch, William M. F. Petrie

Two Hieroglyphic Papyri from Tanis

Heinrich Karl Brugsch, William M. F. Petrie

Two Hieroglyphic Papyri from Tanis

ISBN/EAN: 9783337406783

Printed in Europe, USA, Canada, Australia, Japan

Cover: Foto ©Andreas Hilbeck / pixelio.de

More available books at **www.hansebooks.com**

EXTRA MEMOIR OF
^
THE EGYPT EXPLORATION FUND.

TWO HIEROGLYPHIC PAPYRI FROM TANIS.

I.—THE SIGN PAPYRUS (A SYLLABARY), BY F. LL. GRIFFITH.

II.—THE GEOGRAPHICAL PAPYRUS (AN ALMANACK), BY W. M. F. PETRIE.
WITH REMARKS BY PROFESSOR HEINRICH BRUGSCH.

FACSIMILES AND INTRODUCTORY REMARKS.

--

PUBLISHED BY ORDER OF THE COMMITTEE.

LONDON:
TRÜBNER & CO., 57 & 59, LUDGATE HILL, E.C.

—

1889.

LONDON:
PRINTED BY GILBERT AND RIVINGTON, LIMITED,
ST. JOHN'S HOUSE, CLERKENWELL ROAD, E.C.

CONTENTS.

———•———

I. THE SIGN PAPYRUS.

By F. Ll. Griffith.[1]

This papyrus is the first native list of hiero-glyphics that has come down to us from ancient times. It is at once highly interesting and very disappointing. It is of the highest interest as being the only document bearing upon the system by which the Egyptians arranged and taught their huge syllabary. It is disappointing, because we find so little system in it. We should have expected a more logical arrangement of the signs, and more method in naming them; more indication of a fixed order in the alphabetical signs, if not some correspondence with the order of that alphabet which the Phoenicians seem to have borrowed from the Egyptians. From the considerable care with which the list has been prepared, and from its extent, we must suppose that if any rigid method was customary it would have been adopted here; and we are driven to conclude that the Egyptians possessed no such system.

Apart from its value in the history of writing, the papyrus forms a kind of dictionary which will give the philologist valuable hints for determining the meaning of many doubtful words.

The collection from which it was selected for publication by Mr. Poole—who first detected

[1] This memoir was written, and the plates drawn, in Nov. 1885. I made some additions in 1886, when my much-regretted friend, Mr. H. T. Talbot, read through the proofs.

the parallel lists of hieroglyphics and hieratic on its dark pages—is a very considerable one. Some account of the discovery and condition of these papyri, the first obtained in the Delta, may be interesting.

In the spring of 1884, after the survey of the temple area at Sân had been completed, Mr. Petrie turned his attention to the remains of the town encircling it. It struck him that those houses which had been burnt would yield the most profitable results. In case of fire, the owner would snatch up his valuables, leaving the mass of the household property to the flames. The house falling in would cover them with rubbish, from which the unfortunate man would not care to disinter his burnt and broken jars, tools, and papyri. The reddened earth and bricks betray the site to the modern explorer, and a few days' work in the friable and easily-searched rubbish yields him all that the fire has spared. Putting this theory into practice, Mr. Petrie obtained a large collection of pottery and other antiquities, together with a number of papyri. In some cases the documents stowed away in a corner of the house had been damaged beyond recovery. Lying in a basket on the mud-floor the damp had reached them, and with the weight of rubbish on the top, had reduced them to a mass scarcely distinguishable from the clay beneath; and although the writing was still partly legible, it was found impossible to remove even fragments of any value. Others, although not actually burnt, had been baked

B

violently by the heat of the conflagration, and lying amongst less compact rubbish, had better resisted the destructive damp of the marshes. A number of these were recovered and brought to England. They are of a yellowish-brown colour, soft, and with a tendency to turn to dust on being handled. Large flakes, however, can be separated from some of them, so as to leave the written surfaces successively visible, but the flakes cannot be preserved. Copies must therefore be made of these by an Egyptologist standing by as they are gradually taken to pieces. Amongst them are several minutely written demotic documents, with the red and black ink well preserved.

The most satisfactory class in the collection are those that have been carbonized. Some of these, too, have become a homogeneous mass that cannot be induced to flake. Of others little remains but white ash. A few, though flaking easily, are of too thin a substance to be preserved, while a large number, probably, as Mr. Petrie suggests, through the use of a vegetable ink, have lost the writing wholly, or it is too faded to be read. This, however, may be due to the practice of erasing a text when no longer required, to give place to a new one. Notwithstanding all this, Mr. Hunt, of the MSS. Department of the British Museum, to whom the task of mounting the papyri was intrusted (and to whom great praise is due for the care and discrimination with which he has executed it, under Mr. Petrie's directions), has filled sixty frames, of an average surface of two square feet, with fragments of 156 papyri. Some of these are mere scraps, and will probably afford no information, but many are of real value, not only giving a connected sense, but containing matter of high interest, as the two specimens copied by Mr. Petrie and myself will show.

The papyrus fragments have been mounted in frames formed by two sheets of glass, held apart by a thin piece of cardboard round the edges to allow for wrinkles in the papyri; both sides of which can thus be seen. The fragments are kept in place under the glass with shell-lac. The task of mounting the papyri was a simple, although a delicate one. The rolls had been crushed flat, and so consisted of a series of flakes, each the same breadth as the crushed roll. The flakes were removed with a paper-knife from each side of the roll alternately, the order thus obtained being fairly correct. In some cases it was found more convenient to divide the roll in the middle, and, beginning from the centre, to take flakes alternately from each half.

Some of the papyri were found to have been rolled tightly round a piece of reed, others were without this central support. Some still showed the thread with which they had been tied. The papyrus described in this report seems to have been wrapped round with a piece torn from another document, while the geographical papyrus had a religious text on a separate sheet rolled up with it.

Mr. Petrie found some papyri associated with glazed pottery figures of the style of the thirtieth dynasty. But most of those that have been mounted are of Roman date. In these the writing is in linear hieroglyphic, a small and neat hieratic, demotic of several styles—from large and coarse to fine and very minute,—and Greek. The Greek papyri give the names of several emperors, the name of a private person, Hadrian, being perhaps the latest indication of date in the collection.

The best preserved papyri are stiff, with a shiny surface, as if blackleaded; the ink is black, or yellowish where it was originally red. They have been thoroughly charred; most in fact have had the largest part burnt away. All, except two, are from the house of Bakakhuiu, whose numerous rolls contained religious as well as legal texts. Some were, perhaps, connected with the plans of a new or restored temple. The geographical and other lists in the papyrus, which Mr. Petrie has copied (No. 103), with the scraps of a similar one (Nos. 130 and 131), where the entries of nomes, feasts, marshlands, &c., are corrected by notes in minute hieratic at the foot,[1] and especially the columns of hieroglyphics in papyrus 118, in which the gods grant divine gifts to a king or emperor, whose cartouche is unfortunately left blank, seem as if they were sketches and notes to be expanded on some temple-wall at Tanis.

The Sign Papyrus was found in the house of Bakakhuiu. It fills two large frames, and forms one of the most complete documents in the collection. The crushed roll has been burnt at the lower end, the fire spreading up one side, so that while the top is nearly complete, the twenty-five pairs of fragments taper to a point at the bottom throughout. The papyrus was divided into thirty-three pages, which are not numbered, but the order of which can be found from a comparison of the arrangement of the fragments as mounted with the order to be obtained from their form and contents. Only one fragment still remains without a likely place.

As arranged in the frames, the pairs of fragments are in most cases kept together, but the order of the successive pairs is often the reverse of the correct one, and at the beginning of the papyrus, through no fault of the mounter, there is considerable confusion. A succession may be noticed from the large flakes two inches across, which come from the outside of the roll, where the fire burnt them unequally, to the narrow but little damaged strips from the centre. There is an abrupt change of form in the middle of the fourth page of the final arrangement, the pairs on the right being reversed copies of those on the left of that point, while the first piece to the left is the most fragmentary of all, through crushing. It is evident that this last was the outside fold of the roll, and that the Egyptian owner had turned in the end of the papyrus, probably owing to its being torn, and to prevent damage to the writing at the edge. Two small fragments placed by the side of this page must have belonged to an outside wrapping, for which a piece of papyrus torn from some religious work in hieratic was made to do duty. The beginning of the roll can be recognized in the three fragments which, when placed together, appear doubly forked below. This indicates another turning in of the edge. We may therefore consider that we have the commencement of the roll, since part of the external wrapping even is preserved.

The writing is in many parts easily legible, especially when light is thrown at right angles upon the flakes.[2] Horizontal and vertical lines are, however, difficult to distinguish from the lines of the papyrus, and the play of light on the shiny and irregular surface adds to the difficulty. Six narrow strips at the end, making together about five inches, are blank, and the last two pages have lost much of the writing, probably on account of the tightness of the roll round the stick in that part, causing the flakes to adhere together. There is no writing on the back. The pages follow each other from right to left; the papyrus was rolled from left to right. The thirty-three pages are divided into columns, the first of which contains a row of hieroglyphic signs, enclosed by vertical lines. To the left of them are hieratic transcriptions of the same signs. The remainder of the page contains corresponding groups in hieratic. The width of each page is two inches, that of the hieroglyphic column alone half an inch. The total length of the papyrus as it

[1] Unfortunately, only the lower edges of these papyri are preserved, showing portions of nome-standards, and the rare corrections.

[2] I have to thank Mr. Petrie for helping me over the difficulties of lighting, as also for much assistance in preparing the work for publication. In the copy I have marked the burnt edges with a fringe, as these are of great importance in determining the position of fragments.

existed when rolled up for the last time was therefore nearly six feet.

The number of signs contained in a page seems to have varied. The largest number of which traces are now left in a page is fourteen. From the succession in some of the early pages it seems probable that this was about the original average. The thirty-three pages may then have contained 462 signs, not a large number in comparison with a complete list of hieroglyphic signs. It will be seen that many classes of signs are represented, including a large proportion of the most usual signs that occur in hieratic. Yet no birds, figures of gods, or numerals, occur in the remaining fragments.

As to the order of the signs, the first page is headed by the bee, a royal emblem. Then follows a male child. Figures of men, denoting dignities, are followed by other male human figures extending into page 2. It is possible that the first sign of page 1 is to be considered as the end of a list of divine or royal figures which occupied a page torn off in ancient times. The unplaced fragment (A. 13°) cannot be assigned to this position.

The list was probably preceded by a title, since there is no endorsement to the papyrus, and its loss is to be regretted. It was to prevent further damage to the written portion that the end was turned in, and an extra sheet wrapped round outside.

On page 3 we see figures of women, and seated figures, which are continued to the middle of page 4, where the mummy appears in the hieratic. Page 5 brings us to reptiles and animals, pages 6 and 7 deal with alphabetic signs. At the end of page 7 the series of parts of the human body begin. This is carefully arranged from the head, with eyes, ears, beard, &c., the neck, breast, and back (p. 8), hair and arms (p. 9), fingers, heart, &c. to legs (p. 10). On page 11 we see symbols for flesh and bone, egg, &c. On page 12, legs, horns, and heads of

animals, heads of birds, head of reptile. On page 13, bird's wing, crocodile's tooth (?), followed by the crescent of the moon, figures of sky, stars, and disks, which are continued on page 14. The setting sun leads to the earth and its symbols. From this point regular classification ceases. The remainder of page 14 is devoted to some round and oval objects. Vases appear on the next page, as also on pages 16, 20, 22, and 23; plants on 16, 27, and 31, and so forth. In most cases the signs are connected with those that precede and follow in some way by form, and often fall into groups, but there is no principle observed throughout. I have noticed no instance in which the hieratic form can be supposed to have influenced the arrangement, nor does phonetic value have any share in it, either with regard to similarity of sound or number of syllables. I am inclined to think that the alphabetic signs are separated, not so much for phonetic reasons, as for the different part they played from the rest of the signs of the hieroglyphic system. The order of the Egyptian alphabet, as given in the papyrus, has been no standard for the arrangement of the remainder of the signs.

The hieroglyphics in the papyrus are sometimes very delicately drawn. The reptile's head (p. 12) in the original is a good instance of Egyptian skill, but the scribe has made a slip in the figure of the priest, where the water pours over his back instead of his hands.

As to the hieratic signs, they are carefully written in a peculiar, rather small hand. In the second column the scribe has written the hieratic equivalent of the hieroglyphic sign alone. In a few cases, however, he has substituted the group in which it usually appears. At page 26. 8. the simple sign is evidently omitted by error.

The object of the first two columns is clear enough. A parallel list of hieroglyphic and hieratic signs would be as useful to a student of Egyptian writing then as now.

The object of the third column is fairly clear after a little study. The hieratic notes contained in it consist sometimes simply of the completed group of the corresponding sign with its phonetic complement or determinative, as, for instance, 20. 4. ⟨sign⟩ = ⟨sign⟩; 14. 2. ⟨sign⟩ = ⟨sign⟩; sometimes of the phonetic transcription, with the sign as a determinative, e.g. 16. 1. ⟨sign⟩ = ⟨sign⟩. If two values are indicated, they are separated by a point on the level of the bottom of the characters, as for instance 13. 9, where ⟨sign⟩ = ⟨sign⟩ · ⟨sign⟩. Or, again, a phrase of several groups may occur, as 13. 11 ⟨sign⟩ = ⟨sign⟩; 8. 1, ⟨sign⟩ = ⟨sign⟩; 8. 2, ⟨sign⟩ = ⟨sign⟩.

This third column seems to contain names by which the signs were ordinarily known, or might be recognized. It evidently was not intended as a syllabary of phonetic values, for in so many cases the sign is not transcribed, while in others the note is expanded into a phrase; nor a glossary of ideographic meanings, for the alphabetic signs which are included have no such meaning; nor again of explanations of the form, that is, very condensed descriptions of the sign, for in the group ⟨sign⟩ = ⟨sign⟩, 10.2 ⟨sign⟩ has no known concrete meaning. We might, however, possibly translate 'the finger pointing.' This would be a new shade of meaning for the root ⟨sign⟩, and is unnecessary. Again in ⟨sign⟩ = ⟨sign⟩, ⟨sign⟩ cannot in any way be a description of the sign ⟨sign⟩, and we are prevented from translating 'the disk of day,' or 'in the day-time' (itself an awkward expression), by the point dividing the words.

Nor, again, are these groups a series of notes illustrating the use of the sign in practice. For the particular sign does not always appear in them; as, for instance, p. 1. 4, ⟨sign⟩ = ⟨sign⟩.

On the other hand, a need must have been felt in Egypt of some means of distinguishing hieroglyphic signs viva voce, both in the schools and in ordinary life. Names must therefore have been attached to the immense hieroglyphic syllabary, and taught with care, from the earliest times. If we consider the third column as devoted to the names of the signs, we shall find a fair explanation.

The following are some of the commoner forms of the names; many can be interpreted in several ways:—

I. If contained in one group, they are either (1) the simple *names* of objects represented by the signs as pictures; as page 14. 3, ⟨sign⟩ = ⟨sign⟩, 'earth;' 12.1, ⟨sign⟩ = ⟨sign⟩ 'haunch:' the mirror is apparently called ⟨sign⟩ ? 'see face,' p. 27. 6. The scribe has not always taken the trouble to repeat the sign in such cases as ⟨sign⟩ = 'ah,' p. 29. 5; ⟨sign⟩ = 'set,' p. 25. 2.

(If the object occurs in pairs, the name of the sign is in the dual, as ⟨sign⟩ = ⟨sign⟩ 'sandals,' ⟨sign⟩ = ⟨sign⟩ 'the eye-brows,' ⟨sign⟩ = ⟨sign⟩ 'the lips,' p. 11. 6, p. 8. 3 and 5.)

(2) Or the group may be derived from the ideographic or symbolic meaning of the sign, or that indicated by the action in the case of human beings; as, ⟨sign⟩ = ⟨sign⟩ 'sit,' p. 3. 12; ⟨sign⟩ = ⟨sign⟩ 'adoration,' ⟨sign⟩ = ⟨sign⟩ 'gods.'

Two groups may form one word ⟨sign⟩ = ⟨sign⟩, p. 15. 2; ⟨sign⟩ = ⟨sign⟩ p. 24. 3.

These names are derived from the ideographic meaning of the signs.

II. If the name is contained in two or more groups, it may be (1) a compound name of the object formed by a noun and participle :—

⟦hieroglyphs⟧ 'wood-cut,' p. 17. 1.

⟦hieroglyphs⟧ 'weeping-eye,' p. 8. 1.

⟦hieroglyphs⟧ 'inverted-eye,' p. 8. 2.

In this class of name the second member distinguishes two of a class by detail of the form.

Or it may be (2) formed by a noun followed by another in the genitive, as—

⟦hieroglyphs⟧ 'the disk of the sun,' p. 13. 11.

⟦hieroglyphs⟧ 'the lip or crescent of the moon,' p. 13. 4, opposed to ⟦hieroglyphs⟧ 'the lips.'

Here the second group marks distinction by the derivation of the sign.

Or it may (3) consist of two groups separated by a point—

⟦hieroglyphs⟧ 'the disk, *hru*,' where the latter group distinguishes this from other disks by its phonetic value; thus also ⟦hieroglyphs⟧ hieratic ⟦hieroglyphs⟧ 'the finger, *qemam*,' opposed to ⟦hieroglyphs⟧ hieratic ⟦hieroglyphs⟧, the finger simply ⟦hieroglyphs⟧

The name-forms seem to have no reference to the classes of signs as alphabetic, ideographic, determinative, &c.

As to the date of the papyrus, there is no doubt of its having been written in the Roman period. It is not a direct copy of an earlier list, although it may be an adaptation and selection from a list of Ramesside times.

The spelling of the words agrees with the Roman date attributed to the papyrus; and as to the grammar, although the article does not occur, except perhaps in p. 30. 7. the participial forms used in the compound names are not found, I believe, in inscriptions or papyri earlier than the eighteenth dynasty. These names, however, may belong to a popular dialect in which such forms can have existed at a much earlier period, and it must be remembered that they were probably never written down except for occasional teaching in schools. There is no careful principle in their construction. Probably no complete list was ever drawn up, and perhaps it was not until the decline of the ancient learning in Roman times that such written lists were made at all. The names probably embody ancient and original ideas about the form, meaning, and sound of the signs, as for instance ⟦hieroglyphs⟧; but in course of time, being transmitted principally by word of mouth, they became much modified in form.

The Transcription will be seen to be incomplete, but I have thought it right to add it, partly because the work will fall into the hands of some who are not acquainted with hieratic, but who will be interested to know something of the contents of the third column in order to draw their own conclusions about the papyrus; partly also to justify my reading of the original to those who are familiar with the script. It also affords a convenient means of adding such notes as seem required. M. Naville was able to spare several valuable hours during his short stay in England in 1885 for the tedious task of comparing the first pages of my copy with the original. The corrections and suggestions which he made are noted in the course of the Transcription.

I.

1.			Bee. (Sign of royalty in Lower Egypt.)
2.			Human being as child.
3.			Chief.
4.			Elder.
5.			Prince.
6.			Ruler.
7.			Old age.
8.			High.
9.			Fall.
10.			Speak.
11.			Adore.
12.			Turn back.
13.			Build.

II.

1.		
2.		lost
3.		„
4.		
5.		„ ‘
6.		

III.

1.			Female figure.
2.			Lower Egypt.
3.		or	Suckle.
4.			Priestess.
5.	(?)	(?)	Person, people seated (??)
6.			Person eating, speaking.
7.	* 2		Woman carrying.
8.		lost.	
9.	(female)		Call.
10.		lost.	
11.		......	Sit (?)
13.	(female)		Sit.
14.		lost.	

IV.

1.			Companion.
2.			Guardian.
3.	* 3		Pure.
4.	( )	( )	Falling.
5.	( )		Great statue. 4
6.	( )	( )	Mummy.

[1] I owe the determination of the first two characters to M. Naville.
[2] The reading of this sign was suggested by M. Naville.
[*] The hieroglyphic sign in the original is incorrect.
[4] M. Naville's determination.

IV.			
7.		〇	
8. [1]		(??) or	
V.			
1.			Tadpole (?).
2.			
3.			Body.
4.		(⊝)	Uraeus.
5. [2]		(⊝ ꟽ) (?)	Snake.
6. [3]		(ꟽ) (?) or (ꟽ) (?)	Worm.
7.	ꟽ	(ꟽ) (?)	
8. [3]		lost	
9.		,,	
10.		,,	
11. [4]		,,	
12.		,,	
13.		,,	
14.		,,	
VI. [5]			
1.		(?)	Mouth of human being.
2.			String twisted, tied.

[1] Of the fragments of this page, IA 2, was evidently on the outside of the roll, while the piece IA 3 to the end of the papyrus was turned in. This is therefore the most likely place for a lost page; moreover there is no distinct connection between the fragments IA 1 and 2. IA 3 and 4 are probably portions of the outer wrapping.

[2] N.B. Alphabetic signs.

[3] M. Naville's suggestion, which is certainly correct.

[4] M. Naville reads this ; I think however that the calf is correct.

[5] The continuity of pages 5 and 6 is not certain. This list of alphabetic signs includes four (?) , ∪, , and (?) that might have been placed in the next series of parts of the human body. On the other hand, two alphabetical

VI.

3.	⊔		The arms " ka."
1.	(ℰ)		.... measuring line.
5.	(𓆓)		Measuring line.
6.	(𓂋)		
7.	(—)		Bolt.
8.		lost	
9.			

signs, and, are included in the animal series preceding. The scribe seems to have aimed at making each list as he came to it complete at the expense of the others. In the alphabetic list no stringent order, phonetic or otherwise, is observed, nor does the arbitrary order here adopted influence in any way the arrangement of the other signs.

On page 7 fourteen signs remain. If we take this as the original number on page 6, and assume that the alphabetic list begins at the top of page 6, we obtain fourteen on page 6, and ten on page 7 = 24 alphabetic signs. There are twelve certain signs remaining in the hieroglyphic and first hieratic column. These arranged in the usual phonetic order are as follows: . Of the remaining twenty-six signs that are usually considered alphabetic, or might have stood in the list, namely, the two reptiles and have appeared on the preceding page: the birds and animals, five in number, may perhaps be relegated to the bottom of pages 4 and 5: is equivalent to on the last page: five others, and may be replaced as in the transcription.

Thirteen signs remain, namely, and. Of these the first may well have been omitted, the third seems to occur on page 17, the sixth may not have been considered alphabetic. The last is doubtful and unlikely in this position. The total would thus be twelve certain + five probable + nine = twenty-six, or two more than the estimate. These two may have found a place at the bottom of pages 5 and 6, making fifteen signs to a page.

With the fragments of page 8 is included one, 1 A 13°, with remains of five hieratic groups. It is evidently broken from the right hand fragment of a pair. The groups may perhaps be transcribed as follows:—

1.	(𓃀 (?))		Leg (?)
2.			Wooden instrument used in winnowing (?)
3.	(⊏⊐ (?))		Lake, water.
4.	(𓏏𓏏 (?))		Lotus ...
5.	(𓂝𓂝)		

This is rather a *tour de force*, but the fragment is a puzzle. It certainly does not belong to page 8; but being mounted with it, it should be placed near it, nor can any place be found for it with the other fragments. Also a page near the outside would be more probably damaged and lost than those inside, and this part of the papyrus was near

VII.

1.	𝄞		𝄞	Water plant.
2.	▭		▭	Stomach.
3.	⬇		lost.	
4.	▤		„	
5.	▬		„	
6.	⬠		„	
7.	○		„	
8.	◙ or ◠		„	
9.	⌇		„	
10.	◁		„	
11.	🐍		„	
12.	⚲		„	
13.	◁▭		„	
14.	◁▭		„	

the outside of the roll (*cf. supra*). A right hand fragment would here contain the name column. On the whole, it seems probable that the fragment is the last remainder of a lost pair to be inserted between 4-5 or 5-6. If we look upon the fragments on the left of page 4 (i.e., starting from 1 A 2) as consecutive, and take the known measurement of two inches to a page, we find that between the first and second pairs three-quarters of an inch has been burnt away; between the next two, a quarter of an inch; between the next, one-eighth or thereabouts; while the next pairs practically join. If, however, we allow that a pair has been lost between the first and second, the proportion in the gaps will be more nearly equalised, say $\frac{5}{8}$, $\frac{3}{8}$, $\frac{1}{4}$, $\frac{1}{8}$, 0. At least this proves that there is a possibility of inserting a pair between pages 5 and 6. Also, if we attempt to place it near the beginning of the papyrus, it must be alphabetical, for there is no indication of any other category into which it might fall in any of the early pages. And if it is alphabetical, it must precede page 6, for at page 7 another series begins. But supposing that it precedes page 6, and therefore corresponds partly to fragments 1 A 3 and 1 A 6, it forms part of the first of two lost pages of fourteen signs each at least, of which the right hand one contained alphabetic signs which were continued into page 7. There would indeed be room enough for all the birds and animals belonging to the alphabetic section, and much more besides. Altogether the small fragment is a puzzle.

At page 7, No. 11, the series of parts of the human body begins.

VIII.

1.			Eye weeping.
2.			Eye inverted.
3.			The eyebrows.
4.			The ears.
5.			The lips.
6.			The tongue.
7.			Tooth, the teeth (?)
8.			(?)
9.			(?)
10.			(?)
11.			Beard.
12.			Throat.
13.			Breast.
14.			Back-bone.

IX.

1.			Ribs.
2.			Lock of hair.
3.			Hair (?)
4.			
5.		lost.	
6.			
7.		lost.	

IX.

8.		lost.	
9.		„	
11.		„	
12.	(?)	„	
13.		„	

X.

1.			Finger.
2.			Finger *qmam* (see p. 6, col. 1, line 26).
3.			Thumb (?), claw.
4.			Arms grasping, embracing.
5.			Chest (?), shoulder (?), neck (?).
6.			Heart.
7.			Heart (?) . . .
8.			Flesh (?).
9.		(?)	Urinare.
10.			Testicles.
11.			Vulva.
12.			Leg.
13.			Leg . . .
14.		lost.	

¹ This looks like a false concord; but probably ... is to be read ... unless *ankhpt* is an independent phrase.

XI.

1.			Flesh.
2.			Bone.
3.			Fat.
4.	(?)	(?)	
5.			Egg.
6.			Soles of feet (sandals).
7.		[1]	Dog.
8.		[1]	Pig (?) dog (?).
9.			
10.		[2]	Eye of Horus (hawk).

XII.

1.			Haunch, foreleg (?), shoulder (?).
2.			Leg, *nem.*
3.			Halter.
4.		lost.	
5.			
6.	(?)	,,	
7.			
8.			
9.			
10.			

[1] This looks as if *ån* might be a root-word = hide or tail.
[2] M. Naville showed me the connection of these signs, which fixes the position of the small fragment.

XII.

11.	lost.	lost.	
12.		"	
13.		"	

XIII.

1.			Year.
2.			Wing.
3.			Crocodile's tooth (?).
4.			Lip (crescent) of the moon.
5.			Sky.
6.		(sic) (sic) (?)	Sky rising; (?).
7.			Sky raining.
8.			Sky and star.
9.			Disk *hru*.
10.			Radiancy.
11.			Disk of the sun.
12.			Moon.
13.	( ) (?)	...	Moon (crescent).

XIV.

1.			Radiant disk.
2.			Horizon.
3.			Land.
4.	(o o o)		Three grains of sand; three

[1] This word I owe to M. Naville, who collated the copy to the end of page 14.

XIV.

5.	(x ?)		Land *áfb*.
6.	(?)	(?)	Foundation.
7.			
8.		lost.	
9.	( )		*Sep* (a kind of cake).
10.	(o ?)	(!)	Cycle.
11.		lost.	
12.		...... (?)	

XV.

1.		(?)	Canopy.
2.			Embalmed.[1]
3.			Gods.
4.		lost.	
5.		....	

XVI.

1.		[2]	House.
2.			Fields, *or* field.
3.			Loaf of bread.
4.			Tie of linen.

---

[1] *i.e.*, duly buried and therefore *deified*, being assimilated to Osiris. This notion is common in the religious texts.

The name of the hatchet *neter* means god, but this word was no doubt required for another sign. Why the above expression was chosen for the name of the hatchet sign is not easy to understand, since the hatchet seems to have no connection with burial; probably the notion of 'hatchet' was lost in that of 'god,' and perhaps in common parlance a deceased person was spoken of as the god, or neter, so and so, where in inscriptions we find *maä kheru*. Granting this, the commonest application of the word *neter* furnished a name for the sign ; but I know of nothing to support the view that *neter* was generally applied to deceased persons. (For the exact meaning of *neter*, see Mr. Renouf's Hibbert Lectures, 1879.)

[2] An important transcription, which however scarcely settles the question as to the reading of the sign.

XVI.

5.		(?)	Hide . . .
6.			Vase.
7.			Libation vase.
8.		(?)	Bunch of herbs.
9.			Bunch of flowers, reeds (?)
10.		¹	*Ha*, papyrus.
11.			Thicket of papyrus, *meh*, or *ádhu*-plant.
12.			Thicket of *res*-plant
13.		lost.	

XVII.

1.		²	Wood, cut.
2.			Seed (?) of acacia (?).
3.			Seed of date.
4.		lost.	
5.			Arms *úbauti*.
6.			Fight.
7.	(⊂⊃)		Place.
8.		......	
9.			Milk jug.
10.	(←—)		Subjugate.
11.		(?)	
12.		(?)	Arm presenting.

¹ For the determinative, *cf.* 'papyrus.'

² * Net* masculine like Coptic ⲙⲉ.

D

XVIII.

1.	⌣⌣	⌣⌣	Hill country.
2.	⚱	⚱ ◦	Uast (Thebes).
3.	⚱	...... ⚱∏ ≈	... *userti*, ᴅᴀᴄᴀᴘ vulpes (Brugsch).
4.	⊲	⊲ ◉	Hoe (?) ; the name *mran* would refer to the fastening together of the wood.
5.	⊏⊐	.... ⩓⩓⩓	
12.[1]	⊔	lost.	

XIX.

1.	⊢⊣	⚱ ⌇ ...... ◉ ⌇	.... papyrus.
2.	∿	◯ ◁ ...	Complete.
3.	◠	◯ ⌇ ...	Black.
4.	⩕	⌇⌇ (⌇⩕)	Net, snare.
5.	⩤	⊏ ⌇ ∏ ...	
6.	⚲ hieratic ⚲⚲	⚲⚲ ◉ ⌇	Porter's knot.
7.	⚲	⚲⚲ ⌇ · ∏ (⩥ (?))	
8.	⌇◉	⊏ ⌇ ◉ ◉ (⌇◉)	Utensils, *āu*, *or* writing utensils.
9.	⧹	⊏ ⧹	Knife (*atf*).
10.	⌇	⊏ ⧹	Knife.
11.	⌒	∿ ◦ ◉ (⌣ (?))	Adze.
12.	⚱	⚱ ⌇ ...	East.
13.	⚱	⚱ ...	West.
14.	⚱	lost.	

[1] For remainder, see plate.

XX.

1.			*Cf.* sceptre.
2.		(?)	
3.			Sceptre *áms.*
4.			
5.	(?)		
6.			
7.			Vessels (?) to be full.
8.			Vessels (?), (*id*) to be squeezed out, empty.
9.			Flower vase (?).
10.			
11.			Great.
12.			
13.	(—)		Arrow.

XXI.

1.			*Shenu* or *khenu.*
2.			*Sem* (herb).
3.			Basket of metal worker (?)
4.			Javelin.
5.	(?)		
6.			

From this point many of the groups are difficult, and there would be little gained by further transcription. I will only add the name of the sledge used in conveying stone from the deep-cut quarries ⚒ = ⚒ "jackal," xxix, 1. The phonetic equivalent of this sign is *ba.*

II. THE GEOGRAPHICAL PAPYRUS.

By W. M. F. Petrie.

B.

(*Paper presented to the Committee, July* 23, 1885.)

On my return from Egypt this summer, Mr. Poole showed me some of the papyri which I had brought last year from San, and which, despite their completely charred state, had been satisfactorily unrolled by Mr. Hunt, of the MSS. Department. Among these were two which Mr. Poole saw to be of particular interest. One was a hieroglyphic-hieratic sign-book, of which some three hundred hieroglyphic signs, with their transcriptions and pronunciations written in hieratic, still remain. As Mr. Griffith is now engaged on this, I will leave this on one side. The other papyrus contained parts of a calendar of feasts, and two mentions of the name of Khufu. I at once said that it ought to be published, so that students could work on it without the vast risk of its travelling. As no other copyist was available for such an illegible manuscript, the whole of it being burnt entirely black, I set aside other matters, and have produced a copy of all the fragments, ready for the lithographer. It is hoped that proofs may shortly be in the hands of students; but meanwhile I may give a few notes on the points I have observed, the copying, however, having taken so much time that I cannot attempt to work on the reading.

The original papyrus was about twenty-five feet long, and probably about six inches high; it was rolled up as usual, and both ends and one side of the roll were burnt to white ash, leaving the other side carbonized; hence we only have about ⅓ to ⅔ of the whole length, in a series of separate strips, ·8 to 2·2 inches wide, and each about four inches long, in place of the whole height of the roll. From these I gather that the papyrus was a sort of religious Gazetteer and Calendar, divided into thirteen parts.

Part 1. A list of great festivals, &c., beginning with the new year.

Part 2. A list of the nome capitals in successive columns, naming the sacred bark, sacred tree, cemetery, feast-day, forbidden objects, agathodaimon, land, and lake of each city. The town-names are altogether burnt away. The first four remaining are not identical with any of the Edfu list, though they should, by their position, be Tentyra, Diospolis parva, Abydos, and Panopolis; but the rest are the same as at Edfu (excepting some curious variations), and we still have here Hermopolis, Hibiu, Cynopolis, . . . Memphis, Letopolis, Apis, . . . Busiris, Athribis, Cynopolis, and Sebennytus. Towards the end, however, it appears as if two nomes had been omitted, as there is not space for all the number. The last column gives the title of each of the lines, " name of tree," " name of cemetery," &c.

Part 3. Lists comprising the sacred animals, and apparently arranged according to them. We see the piebald bull, *Hapi*, the black bull, *Ka-ur*, the white bull, *Be-khat*; the ram, monkey, panther, pig, jackal, and the birds follow. Lakes, cemeteries, and sacred trees are also given in connection with some town-names; for instance, the tree Asht is given to Pi-Bast, rectifying an erroneous sign at Edfu.

Part. 4. Apparently mentions various priests and goddesses.

Part 5. Similar to Part 2, giving trees, cemeteries, feasts, forbidden things, agathodaimons, lands, and lakes, of more than fifty places, of which eighteen are preserved; the place-names are all burnt away, and none of the entries have I been able to identify with those in the list of nomes. This may be a list of towns in some district or nome. It also ended with a column naming each class.

Part 6. A list of sacred fish, &c., and deities to which they belong, arranged according to localities.

Part 7. A list of feast days, of deities, and of processions of sacred barks; over a hundred entries originally.

Part 8. Another list of fifty or sixty feast days, not of deities.

Part 9. List of about thirty gods, with various entries to each, arranged alternately east and west.

Part 10. A long address in horizontal columns, naming Khufu.

Part 11. A long address in vertical columns, naming Khufu.

Part 12. A diagram of six hours (?), with text.

Part 13. A long statement dealing with fabulous numbers, as hundreds of thousands, and millions.

We may hope for some interesting results when this shall have been studied in connection with other calendars and geographical lists. It is by the merest chance that this document is not complete, as many other rolls were which I discovered; and it shows us the great importance of the closest attention to papyri, even when found under most unfavourable circumstances. The demotic and hieratic papyri await examination, and many of them are perfect.

THE Geographical Papyrus has not been laid aside during the three and a half years that have elapsed since Mr. Petrie copied it. On the contrary, with his leave I have at various times spent hours, and even days, in verifying the words that occur in it, by means of the Geographical Dictionary, the temple lists, the copy, and the extremely obscure original. At length, in accordance with the wish expressed in Mr. Petrie's report, proofs were sent to Professor H. Brugsch, who returned them covered with annotations, and accompanied by the following letter :—

Monsieur,

Quoique je n'aie en que quelques heures à ma disposition pour examiner les feuilles imprimées que vous avez eu la bonté de recommander à mes examens, je peux vous assurer de *ma plus haute surprise* après avoir jeté le premier coup d'œil sur les textes. Les travaux que j'ai faits pendant presque 40 années pour reconstruire les notions géographiques et calendriques des anciens Égyptiens, ont eu leur précédent ! Un Égyptien vivant à l'époque Romaine, peut-être vers l'époque de la composition du tableau calendrique sculpté sur les murailles du temple d'Esneh, se fut amusé à réunir toutes ces notions et sur le modèle d'un tableau synoptique pour faciliter leur connaissance à ses lecteurs. Mais quel dommage que le papyrus renfermant son travail a dû souffrir par les déplorables lacunes qu'il offre ! Heureusement il en est resté assez pour servir à nous guider sur les idées de l'ancien compositeur et écrivain des divers tableaux. D'après mes observations, qui ne font que corroborer vos propres vues, la composition embrasse les sujets suivants que j'ai traités dans mon Thesaurus (Inscriptt. Astron.) et dans le Dictionnaire Géographique, sans avoir pu pressentir que j'ai eu mon devancier. En voici le résumé :

1er *Tableau.* Liste synoptique des 12 mois de l'année moderne des Égyptiens, avec les noms des fêtes des mois et avec les (noms des ?) heures du jour en ordre consécutif et distribuées, par des motifs que j'ignore, sur les 12 mois en question.

2^d *Tableau.* Les noms des 12 heures de la nuit.

3ème *Tableau.* Les 30 jours de la lune avec les noms correspondants des divinités lunaires de chaque jour.

4ème *Tableau.* Sujet astronomique en rapport avec la lune ou le soleil. Les chiffres ajoutés au mot pour la mesure (schoinos) indiquent, à ce qu'il paraît, des calculs astronomiques.

5ème *Tableau.* Tableaux des nomes de la haute et de la basse Égypte, avec les indications et désignations des arbres sacrés, des Sérapées, des fêtes, des choses défendues, des serpents Agathodémous, des territoires et des terrains inondés.

6ème *Tableau.* Listes et noms des prêtres et prêtresses des sanctuaires situés dans lesdits nomes.

7ème *Tableau.* Liste de métaux (p. ex. ba-ni-pe, la fer) et d'autres minéraux.—Noms des animaux divins vénérés dans un nombre de villes du pays (Apis de Memphis, Mnévis d'Heliopolis, Bakhis d'Hermonthis, le bouc de Mendès, etc.).

8ème *Tableau.* Les fêtes principales fêtées dans le courant de l'année et rapportées aux jours correspondants du calendrier *moderne*.

9ème *Tableau.* Liste de l'hiérarchie à la cour royale d'après les titres des dignitaires, y compris les métiers occupés à la cour.

Le tout se termine par un texte explicatif avec des notions historiques qui méritent une étude particulière sur l'original.

A further contribution from the same hand having been most kindly promised, the publication was delayed for a time. Meanwhile the original was re-examined, proving the correctness of several emendations in the calendrical lists which the illustrious Egyptologist had suggested to me. Unhappily a serious illness intervened, but on his recovery Professor Brugsch was good enough to send me the following valuable and interesting observations.

Plus j'ai étudié les tristes fragments du précieux papyrus de Tanis, plus j'ai trouvé l'occasion de me convaincre que sa valeur principale consiste dans les notions calendriques qu'il renferme. Il confirme ce que j'ai prétendu depuis de longues années dans mes recherches calendriques, en d'autres termes l'existence de deux années, du moins pour la dernière époque de l'histoire égyptienne, dont l'une n'est pas différent de l'année *religieuse*, appelée ordinairement sothiaque, tandis que l'autre, l'année *civile*, est identique à celle qu'on a l'habitude de nommer l'alexandrine. La première commençant à la rentrée de chaque période sothiaque par la date du 1er Thoth, correspondant au $^{19}/_{20}$ juillet du calendrier julien, la seconde par la même date du 1er Thoth, mais cette fois correspondant au $^{20}/_{20}$ août julien, il en résulte nécessairement le nombre de 40 jours qui sépare les dates identiques dans les deux calendriers, le religieux et le civil. Les preuves évidentes nous sont fournies par la trouvaille du papyrus de Tanis.

En étudiant attentivement la série des fêtes, accompagnées de leurs dates, sur les fragments du *Part 7* (planche IV.), on fera la curieuse observation que les fêtes du mois, au commencement des douze mois de l'année égyptienne, ne se trouvent pas à leurs places qu'elles occupent dans les calendriers antiques. C'est ainsi que la fête nommée [glyph] " fête d'Hathor," —nom sous lequel se cache le nom grec Athyr pour le 3ème mois de l'année égyptienne,—est notée sous la date du 1er Choiak, c'est-à-dire au mois suivant celui d'Athyr. En procédant on remarquera également que la fête du mois de Choiak, nommée [glyph] *Kihak*, se trouve inscrite sous la date du 1er Tybi. Un troisième exemple, c'est le dernier conservé sur les fragments du papyrus, se présente au-dessous de la date du mois Mechir ; c'est le groupe encore assez reconnaissable [glyph] qui, à l'époque ptolémaïque, par exemple, (voir mon " Thesaurus " à la page 472), sert à désigner la fête du mois de Tybi, mais non pas celle du Mechir, qui porte le nom de [glyph] *rokh-uêr*. Comme on le voit, les fêtes des mois ne correspondent plus aux mois auxquels elles appartiennent, mais elles les avancent d'un mois entier.

Ce fait, dont on ne pourra pas s'en douter, est corroboré par les fragments du *Part* 1 (à la planche I.), qui ont conservé les derniers restes de la notation des 12

mois de l'an sous la forme connue à l'époque grécoromaine (voir le " Thesaurus," p. 472 suiv.). Mis en rapport avec les 12 heures du jour, le premier mois (Thoth) y porte le nom de [glyph], le seconde celui de [glyph], *Api* (d'où l'appellation de ce mois Pha-*ophi*), le 3ème est indiqué par le groupe [glyph] ; c'est le mois de la déesse Hathor représentée par le scribe du papyrus par l'image d'une vache couchée. Malheureusement les noms des mois suivants ont disparu par suite de la fâcheuse mutilation du papyrus, à la seule exception du dernier (Mesori), qui est appelé très-clairement : [glyph] "mois du commencement de l'an," avec la curieuse remarque qui l'accompagne : [glyph] "descend le soleil " ou peut-être " le jour." Le sens de cette légende est facilement à comprendre ; il s'agit de la descente du soleil vers l'hémisphère inférieure dans la seconde moitié de l'an. En parlant de la déesse Vénus qui déplore Adonis, Macrobe (Saturnall. I., c. xxi.) s'exprime ainsi là-dessus : " quod Sol annuo gressu per duodecim signorum ordinem pergens, partem quoque *hemisphærii inferioris ingreditur*, quia de duodecim signis Zodiaci sex superiora, sex *inferiora* censentur : et cum est *in inferioribus* et ideo dies breviores facit, lugere creditur Dea, etc.

D'après le calendrier alexandrin le mois Mesori embrasse les 30 jours à partir du 25 juillet jusqu'au 23 août jul., ou, les 5 jours épagomènes y compris, jusqu'au 28 août. D'après le calendrier d'Esneh, de l'époque romaine, deux jours avant le commencement du mois Mesori, ou le 29 Epiphi, la fête nommée [glyph] " celle de Sa Majesté " (déesse) était célébrée en l'honneur du lever de la constellation d'Isis-Sothis, lequel anciennement était censée ouvrir la nouvelle année. Le 29 Epiphi en question répond au 23 juillet jul., c'està-dire à la date que les Alexandrins notaient comme jour du lever de l'étoile Sothis à leur époque. C'est confirmé par les témoignages de Théon et de Ptolémée (voir *Unger*, Chronol. de Manéthon, pag. 51). On se convainc donc que le mois de Mesori portait de tout droit le nom de [glyph] "mois de l'ouverture, ou du commencement de l'an." Il remplaçait le mois antique de Thoth et il fut cause que, de cette façon, toutes les fêtes de mois avançaient d'un mois entier les mois de l'ancien calendrier religieux. Il en résulte nécessairement que les dates du papyrus de Tanis sont indiquées d'après l'année alexandrine et que le papyrus doit avoir été composé à une époque où le calendrier alexandrin était d'usage.

Avant de terminer cette petite remarque au sujet des notations calendriques qui se rencontrent sur les fragments dudit papyrus, je voudrais encore fixer l'attention sur le texte, mutilé du reste comme tout ce qui précède, qui est publié sur les dernières planches de la publication. Ce texte débute par une formule bien comme par d'autres spécimens d'un âge de beaucoup antérieur à la rédaction du papyrus. Le compositeur s'adresse à tous ceux qui vivent et qui vivront sur la terre, notamment aux classes savantes des prêtres, pour leur recommander le souvenir éternel de son nom et de ses œuvres. Parmi les dernières, à ce qu'il paraît, la composition du papyrus en question occupa le premier rang. Ayant visité un tombeau appartenant à un dignitaire de la cour et de l'époque du roi *Choufou*-Chéops, il eut la chance d'y découvrir des textes et des objets sacrés de la plus haute valeur. Il cite, par exemple, une coudée de Thot qu'il avait trouvée sur le sol de la tombe. Bref, il ne tarda pas à sauver ces mystères inconnus au monde vivant, en dressant en forme de tableaux les matières sacrées de l'ancienne sagesse sur le papyrus. Il termine son travail par l'expression de son désir qu'en revanche de ses actions, son nom le survive. Malheureusement il n'en est resté que quelques signes à la fin du papyrus.

I have to-day revised portions of the last two plates. Mr. Petrie's division of the papyrus into parts has been preserved, but I have added a running number for the fragments.

F. L. G., *30th Jan.*, 1889.

ERRATUM.

Transcription VI. 2.   Dot only (.) between *hai* and *hbs*.

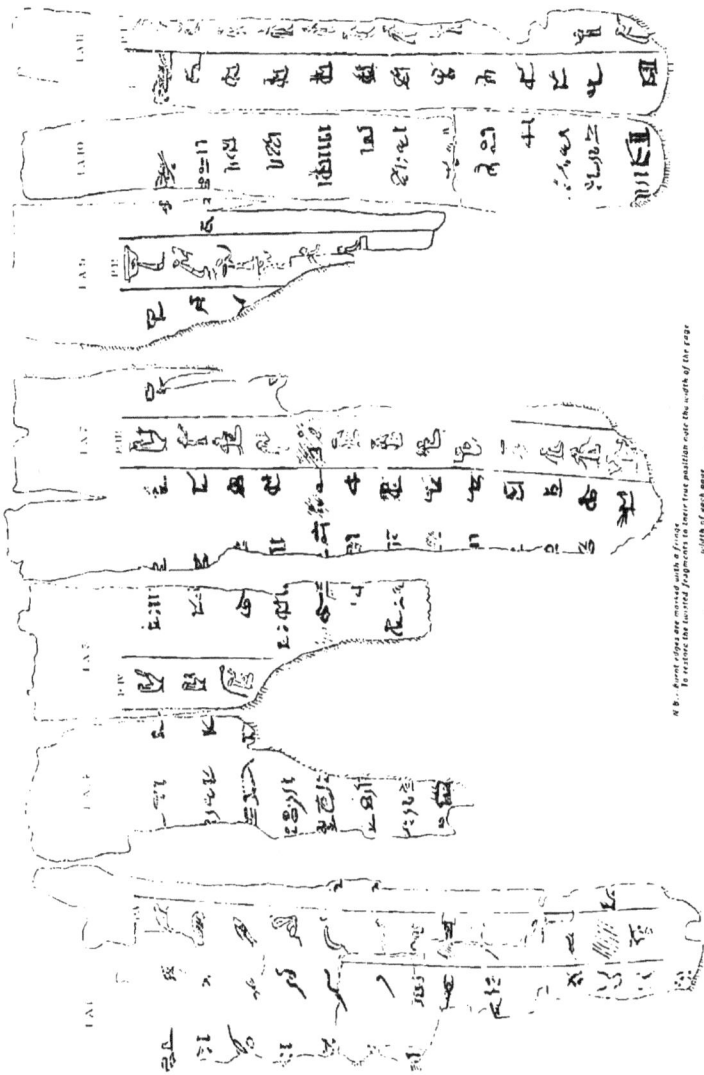

SIGN PAPYRUS

Pl. iv

N.B.— *Burnt edges are marked with a fringe.*
To restore the burnt fragments to their true position rule the width of the page

width of each page

hieratic   hieroglyphic

FIG 46

TANIS, HOUSE 35. PAP 20

SIGN PAPYRUS.

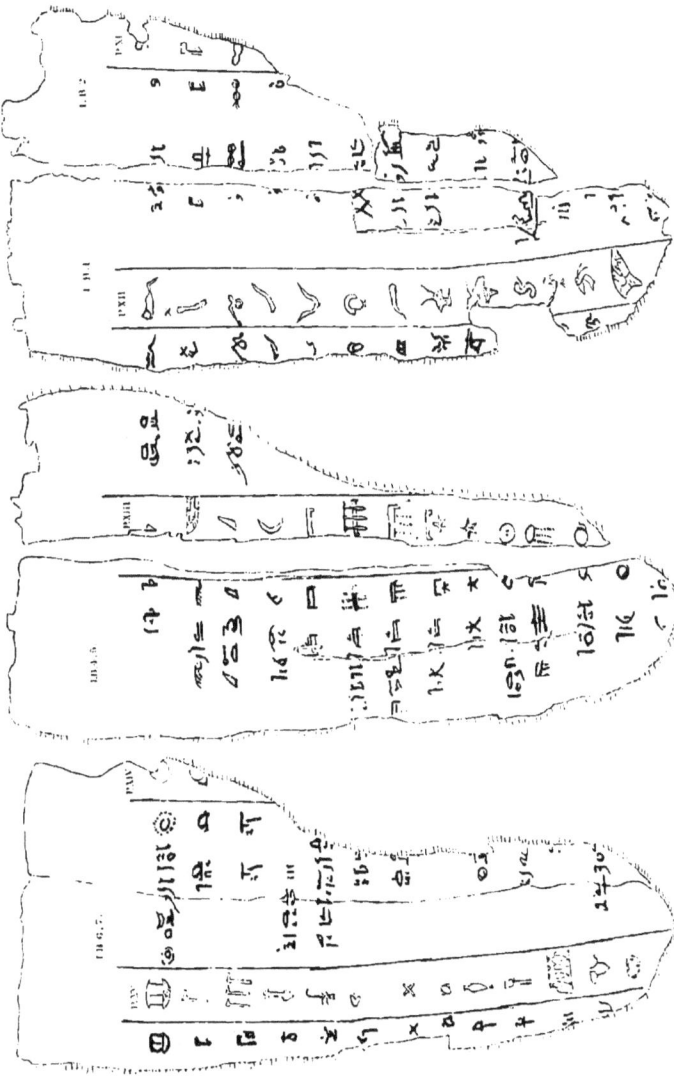

SIGN PAPYRUS.
ṗ. XI-XV.

TANIS. HOUSE 35 PAP. 80.

SIGN PAPYRUS
pp. XV–XIX

TAV. I. HI RS. 33. PAR 45

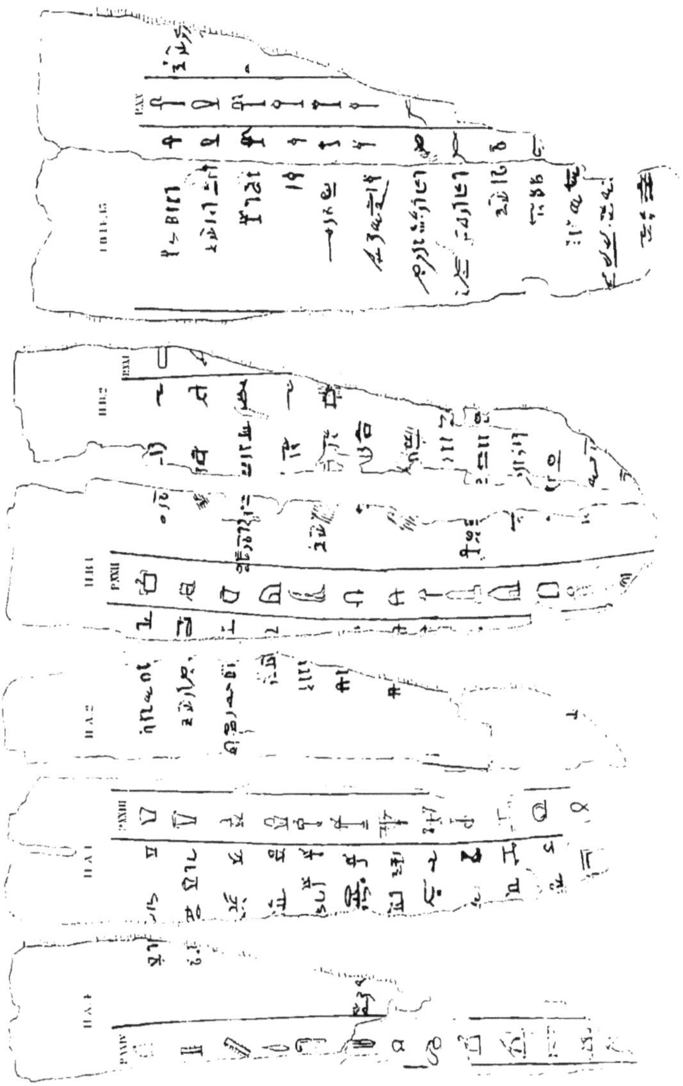

SIGN PAPYRUS.
PP. XXIV–XXVIII.

TANIS. HOUSE 35. PAP. 80.

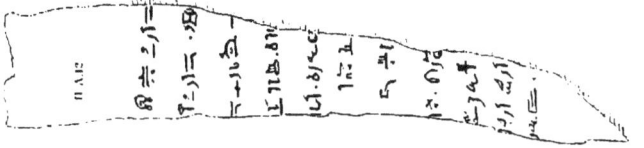
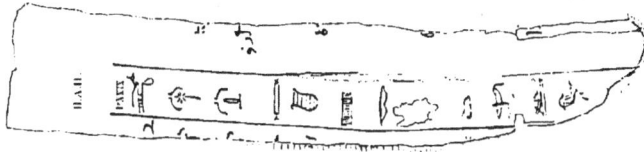

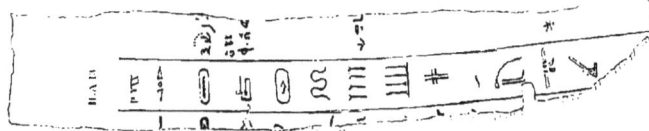
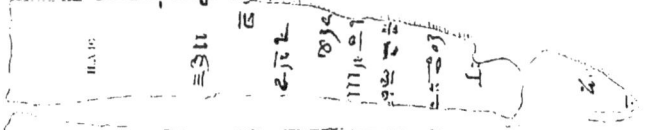
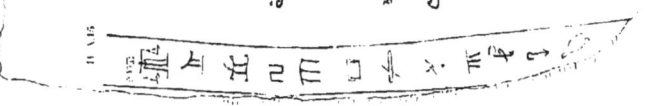

SIGN PAPYRUS.
pp. xxvii-xxxi.

TANIS HOUSE II.

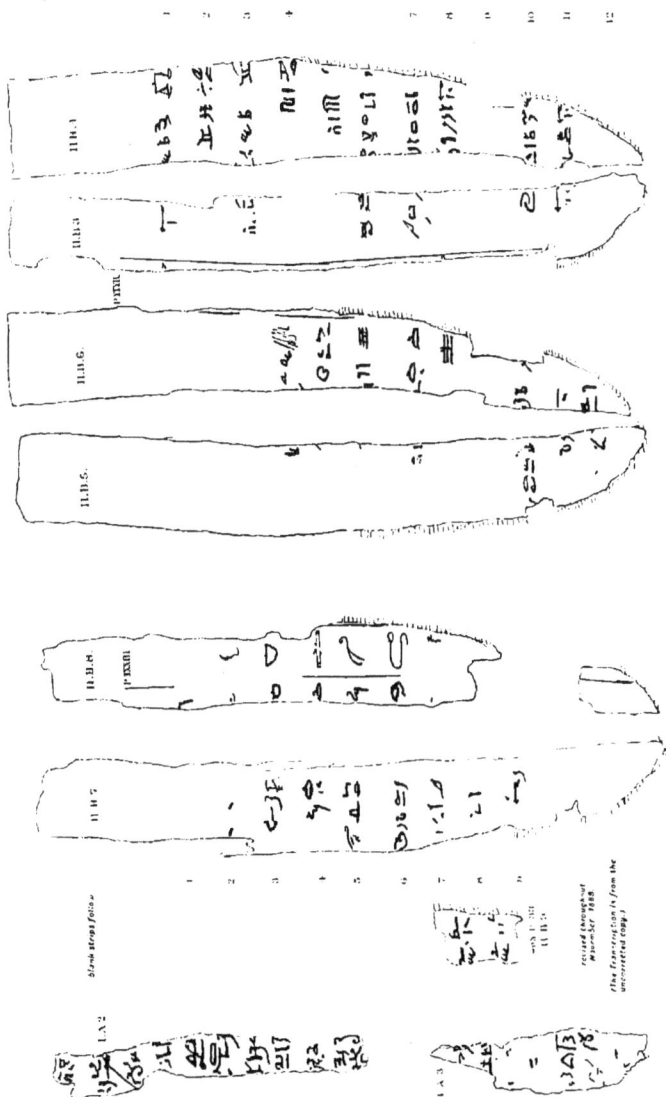

SIGN PAPYRUS.
pp. xxxi-xxxiii.
AND WRAPPER

TANIS. HOUSE 33. PAP. 80.

PL. VIII.

F.LG. del.

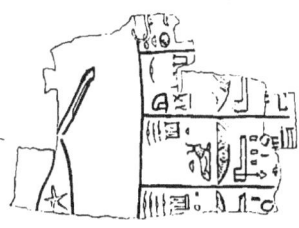

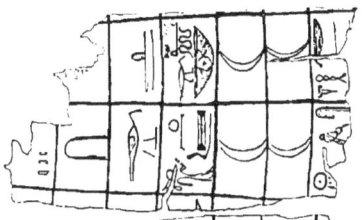

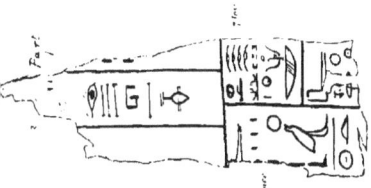

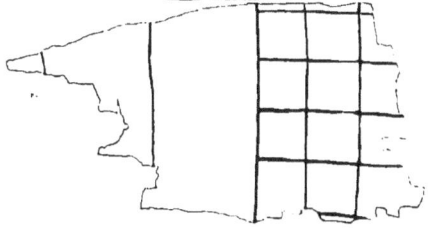

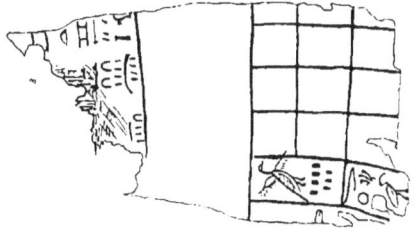

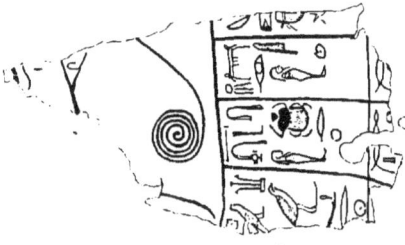

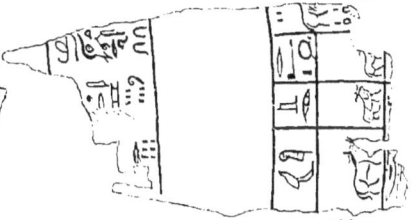

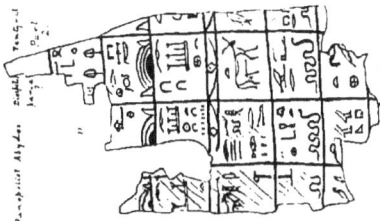

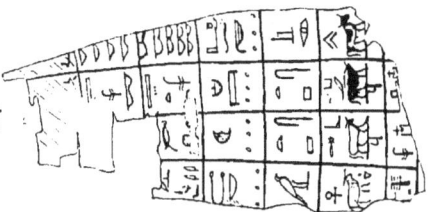

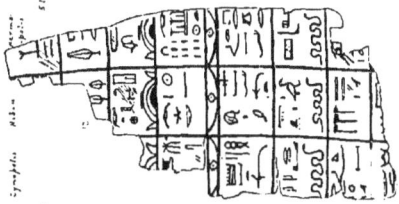

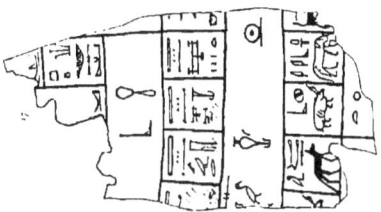

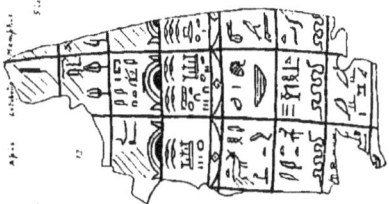

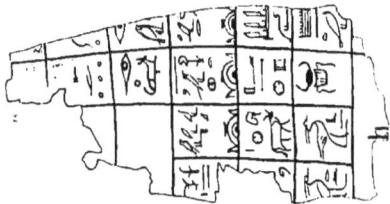

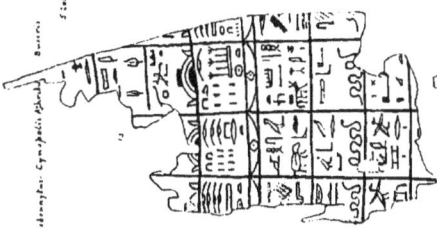

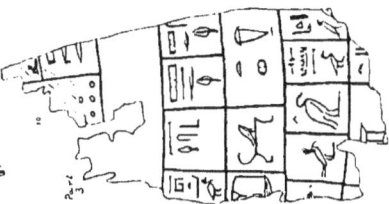

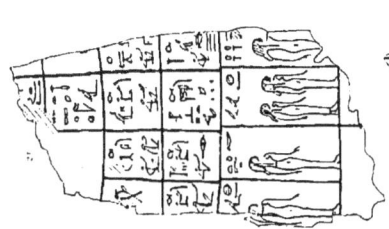
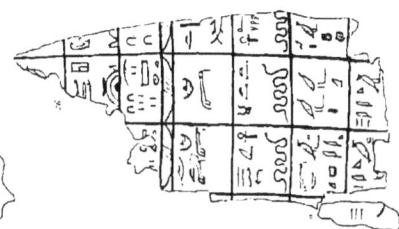
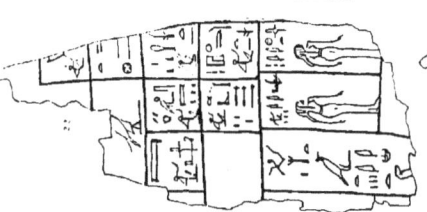
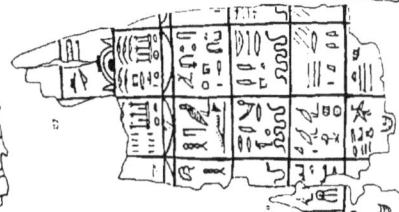
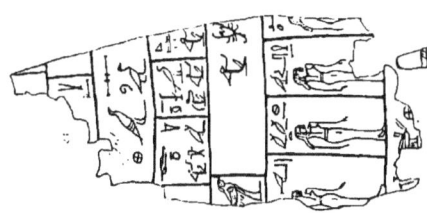
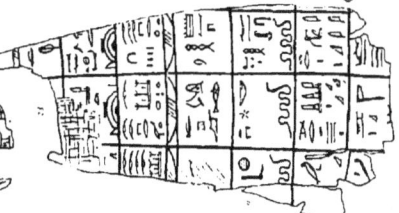
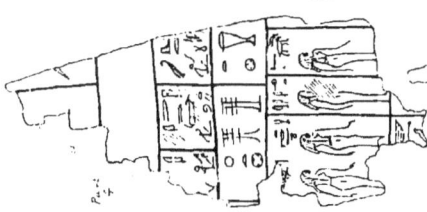
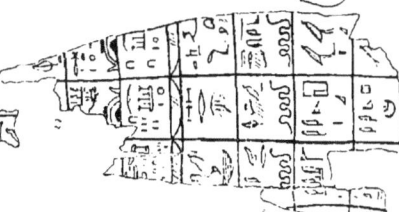
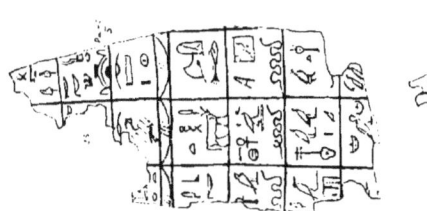

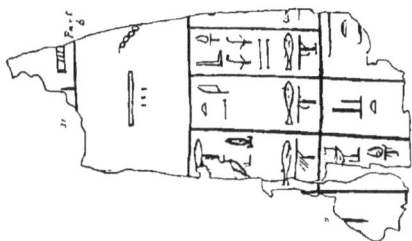
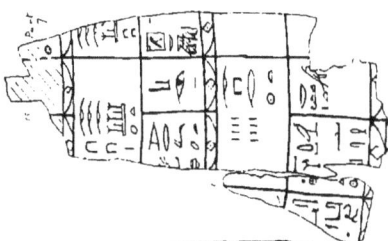
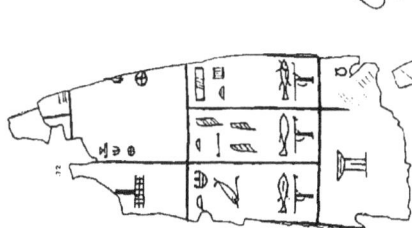
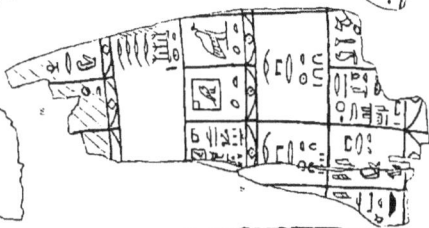

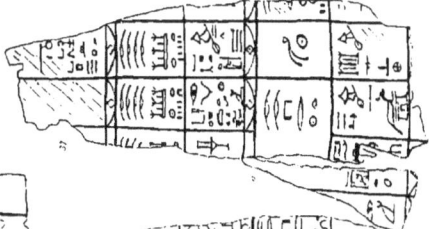
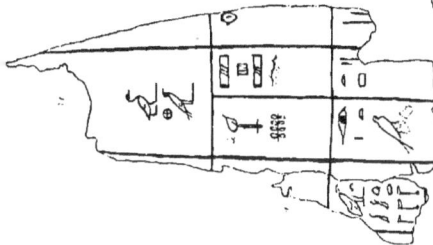

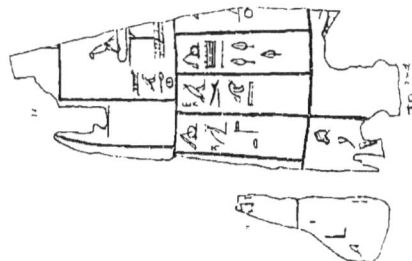

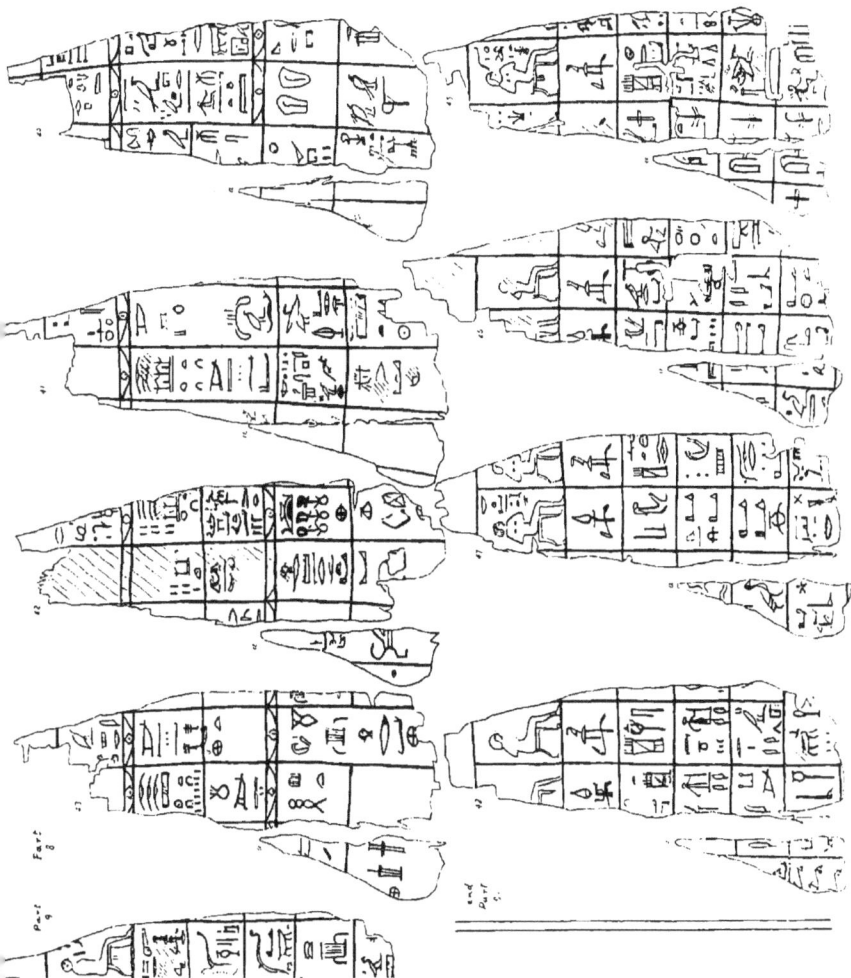

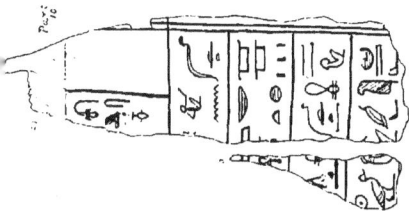

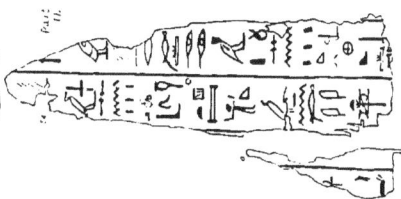

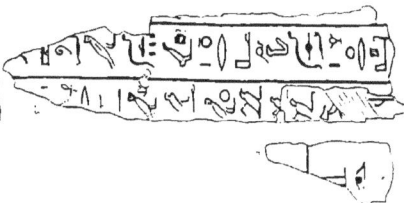

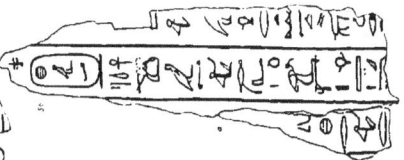

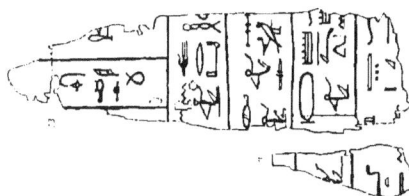

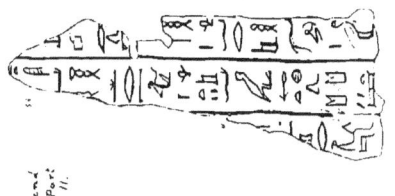

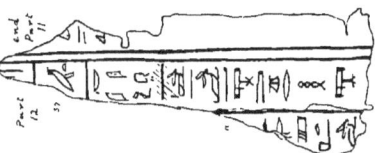

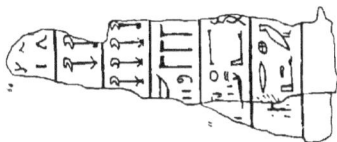

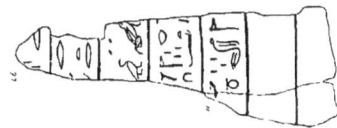

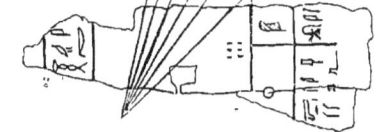

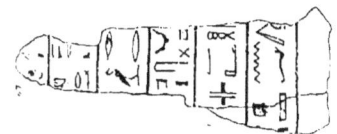

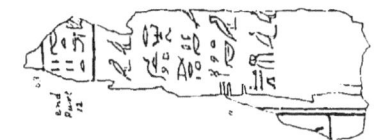

EGYPT EXPLORATION FUND
PUBLICATIONS.

I. *The Store-City of Pithom and the Route of the Exodus.* By EDOUARD NAVILLE. With Thirteen Plates, Two Maps, and a New Autotype Plate of the Store-Cellars of Pithom. Third Edition. 1888. 25s.

II. *Tanis.* Part I. By W. M. FLINDERS PETRIE. With Nineteen Plates and Plans. Second Edition. 1888. 25s.

III. *Naukratis.* Part I. By W. M. FLINDERS PETRIE. With Chapters by CECIL SMITH, ERNEST A. GARDNER, and, BARCLAY V. HEAD. With Forty-six Plates and Plans. Second Edition. 1888. 25s.

IV. *Tanis.* Part II., *Nebesheh (Am)* and *Defenneh* (*Tahpanhes*). By W. M. FLINDERS PETRIE. With Chapters by A. S. MURRAY and F. LL. GRIFFITH. With Fifty-one Plates and Plans. 1888. 25s.

V. *Goshen, and the Shrine of Saft-el-Henneh.* By EDOUARD NAVILLE. With Eleven Plates and Plans. Second Edition. 1888. 25s.

VI. *Naukratis.* Part II. By ERNEST A. GARDNER. With an Appendix by F. LL. GRIFFITH. With Twenty-four Plates and Plans. 1889. 25s.

VII. *The City of Onias, the Antiquities of Tell el Yahûdîyeh, and the Mound of the Jew.* By EDOUARD NAVILLE and F. LL. GRIFFITH. With Twenty-six Plates and Plans. 1890. 25s.

VIII. *Bubastis.* By EDOUARD NAVILLE. With fifty-four Plates and Plans.

EXTRA MEMOIR.

Two Hieroglyphic Papyri from Tanis. Translated by F. LL. GRIFFITH and W. M. FLINDERS PETRIE. With Remarks by Professor HEINRICH BRUGSCH. With fifteen Plates. 1889. 5s.

www.ingramcontent.com/pod-product-compliance
Lightning Source LLC
Chambersburg PA
CBHW031745090426
42739CB00008B/891